Zoltieisms

Alan Zoltie Publishing inc.

ISBN: 978-1-7374122-2-9

Dedicated to my mother and father, Joyce and Jack Zoltie and to my two sisters, Ruth and Barbara.

My son Paul, his very own man, and my daughter Brianna, who inherited my humor but not my inability to be compassionate.

For all your assistance and encouragement PT (Boss!), I thank you.

Zoltieisms Foreword

I'd been writing for about 6 years, mainly poetry, although I'd penned two novels. One novel was a story about an experience I'd had in business, the other, totally fictional, and honestly, not that great. On completion of both books, and after showing them to several literary agents, I was told, in no uncertain terms, "don't give up your day job and come back when you think you have a book that might sell!"

I'd failed English in high school and I never went to college, but all my beliefs, my dreams, my desire to succeed in almost anything I tried, stayed with me from a very early age, an age where people told me I was lazy, useless and incompetent. These beliefs; never to quit and always persist, followed me into my writing career, beliefs that were encouraged and endorsed regularly by my friend and greatest advocate, Paul Trevillion, (www.paultrevillion.com). Paul would often describe my work as "a checkbook, waiting to be written", in other words, he believed that I was on the verge of making millions from my writing, something I never gave a second thought to. I write because I love to express my feelings and humor and above all, my views of all the injustices that surround us on a daily basis. Paul, a world-renowned illustrator, saw it differently. As an artist, he felt my creativity, and he felt it in his heart. Several times over the past 20 odd years, he's suggested to me that my talent and my ability to see our world from a different perspective, be put into print for others to read and digest. I have now written several novels, all true stories, a book about dogs, and now, this book, **Zoltieisms**.

What is a **Zoltieism**?

A **Zoltieism** is a one-line description of a moment, a situation, an injustice, a slice of humor, that will bring uncompromising thoughts into your mind in order that you might try to dissect it's meaning. The very first **Zoltieism** I wrote, "I as a man, am slammed by the thought that everything is temporary except the mark I choose to leave", came to me one afternoon while walking in my local park. At that time, I lived in Northern California and was writing poetry and song lyrics as a hobby. I had written about 4500 of these poems, some good, some great, and some, well, they were just bang average. During the time I had written these poems, one of my goals was to leave some kind of mark on this planet, and not just die to be remembered by a simple gravestone which commemorated the year I was born and the year I died. As I walked around that afternoon, the Zoltieism, (although I hadn't yet decided to name them **Zoltieisms**, mainly because I had no idea there would be anymore to follow the first one), came to me in a very brief moment. I recall typing it into my phone, so I didn't forget it, and after getting back to my office, putting it on a Word document and emailing it to Trevillion. His reaction was, as it always is when I send him something I've written, ecstatic. After we chatted, he challenged me to come up with more and more, and as you will read on the pages that follow, I now have over 400 of what have now become, **Zoltieisms**.

Please sit back, relax and try to comprehend the meaning of each one, not only their true meaning, but the meaning they have to you, in your life, in your situation and with your translation.

Life is strange, often meaningless and always spontaneous. **Zoltieisms** might follow a similar path, although I believe they will have more meaning than you will ever want to admit.

I have other books out on Amazon and they are:

Kennel Hill, a poetic anthology dedicated to our four-legged friends.

The Secret Masseuse, and **The Secret Escort**, both true stories relating to the sex industry in Orange County California.

Cardboard City, a book dedicated to Homelessness, is due out later in 2022.

All proceeds from all of my books go to charities. I do not make a cent from any of my writing.

Alan Zoltie
www.alanzoltie.com

THE MOST IMPORTANT THING IN LIFE
IS THAT NOTHING
IS ACTUALLY THAT IMPORTANT.

I as a man am slammed by the thought that everything is temporary except the mark I choose to leave.

Today's memories will become a shadow, cast by earth's ability to move gently into another day.

If a dog is mans' best friend, should he who befriends a dog be trusted?

Why chase the past when it's the future that always wins?

Definition is the lowest form of vanity, and the highest form of wisdom.

You should never forget where you came from because if you do, you shouldn't have been there in the first place.

Mans natural desire to succeed is greatly surpassed by his desire to destroy everything that is naturally successful.

If actions speak louder than words, why is it that doers are so vocal?

The unlimited is limited by what the brain can comprehend unless limited by unlimited amounts of ignorance.

There are many possibilities in life and only one absolute probability so make the most of all the possibilities before the probability becomes an inevitability

Trying to make sense of senseless moments is making nonsense out of common sense

Boredom is a form of obesity of the mind created by lack of exercise in the brain

IS IGNORANCE A FORM OF ARROGANCE
OR ARE THE ARROGANT TOO IGNORANT
TO HAVE ANY DEGREE OF HUMILITY?

Can you justify an injustice when justice is unjustified?

I'm not morally perfect though I am perfectly moral

Absolute pleasure, derived from pleasurable attributes, attributing to pleasured absolution

I love your front side, backside, inside and out, but most of all I love you by my side

You have to learn to love and then you can love to learn

Hospitality is making your guests feel at home, even though you wish they were back in their own home.

If one person changes your life, are the changes they made life changing?

What happens to the me I was before the me I am now?

It's not the stupid things you remember doing, it's the stupid things you've actually done!

Is gratitude something you learn or is it something that teaches you how to learn?

Is good will something we should all give without conscience or be willing enough to receive without question?

Is success better than failure if failure teaches you how to be successful?

Does worry ever leave a head filled with happiness or is happiness the creator of all worry?

In life, if you take time stop to smell the roses and there is no smell, is it still worth stopping?

THE INEVITABILITY OF THE INEVITABLE
IS NEVER INEVITABLE
UNTIL IS ABSOLUTELY CERTAIN.

Is it better to breathe the fresh air and then stop to smell the roses or stop to smell the roses then breathe in the fresh air?

Do you listen to the aimless thoughts running around in your mind or do you run around aimlessly trying to put thoughts into your mind?

Can you be ambitious if success is taken as a birthright?

If the grass is always greener on the other side, why does the other side never seem to be the right side?

If the sweet smell of success is so pungent, why is it always so hard to sniff?

The only thing perfect in any relationship is 100% trust.

If something is 100% guaranteed, who guarantees the guarantee?

How do you make a dog smell good? Ask another dog!

If a man is described as being all washed up, does that mean he's as clean as a whistle?

If a uniform is a sign of authority, does nudity carry any uniformity that is unauthorized?

If capturing a person's heart makes them a slave to love, does slavery end when that heart is broken?

If the shortest way from point to point is as the crow flies, why do we sit on planes and not crows?

The games we play in our mind are often created by the piecing together of useless information and stray thoughts circulating endlessly inside our heads!

WHEN A BODY CLIMAXES INTO A CRESCENDO
AND THEN FINDS COMPLETE SERENITY,
THE PURPOSE OF LIFE BECOMES ABSOLUTELY CLEAR.

Is it reasonable to assume that the sum of all reasons is a reasonable assumption?

If remorse is the key to sympathy and forgiveness, can you be sympathetic and remorseful but not forgiving?

If it all boils down to the nature of the beast, why does the beast have such a beastly nature?

If variety is the spice of life, are the variable ingredients required for spicing it up, lively? (or life giving)

If it's an ill wind that blows no good, how do we tame that wind to make it better?

It takes excitement and passion to stir up a cause; does it take passionate excitement to cause a stir?

Why is it when we vote for change, everything stays the same, even with change?

Reality is the unfortunate circumstance resulting from all make believe?

Are dreams spawned from reality or does reality create dreamers?

True obedience comes from those who are worthy and not those who are trained

Life is made not by the money we earn but by the love we give!

What's the point in living if you don't take the time to live?

THE APPRECIATION OF WAKING UP EACH MORNING
IS TOTALLY UNDERESTIMATED

Humanity is often too inhumane to be human

Our stupidity seems to always outweigh our ingenuity!

Good judgement comes from experience, and experience comes from bad judgement.

The great thing about freedom is the right to discuss wrongs but right now there are so many wrongs that freedom is debatable!

When you sit down and analyze your life and then realize that its not too much that's important or that really matters, that's what really matters and is important.

The inevitable thing about believing you are infallible, is succumbing to certain inevitable infallibility

Humility can be found resting on the shoulders of fear and complete self understanding

Can the admission of one's own humility only be discovered by other peoples suffering?

Time passes when you're not looking but time passes even if you are, so you have to look really hard to remember where time went

If your mind is spinning round in circles, how do you get it back on a straight line?

An eye-catching dress should never be worn by anyone other than an interesting woman

When you dream in color, realism seems so animated!

IT MAKES LITTLE SENSE WHEN YOU LOSE ALL
SENSE OF SENSIBILITY.

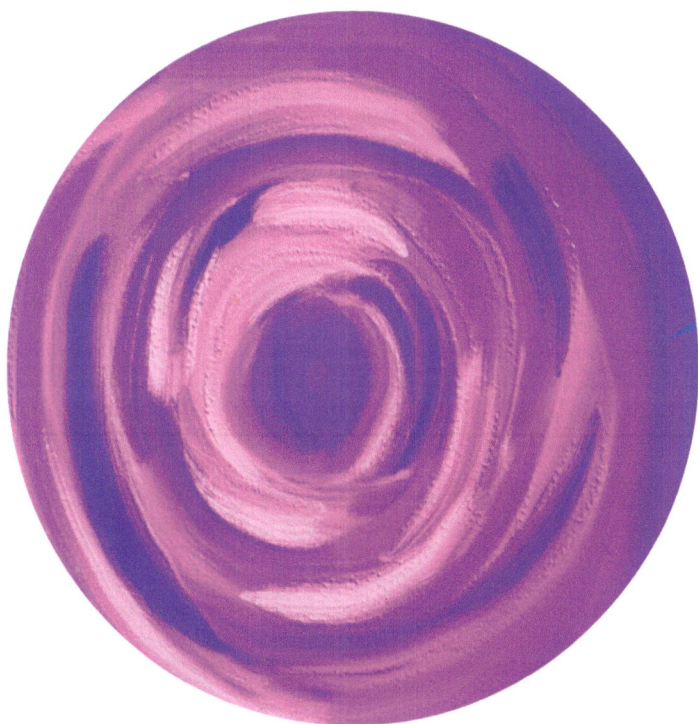

When you dream in color, realism is just pigment in your imagination!

An excuse is nothing but an inexcusable thought to avoid necessity

Life's simplicities are deduced by a state of mind formed by one's age and maturity

Life is one huge big memory, the present, so brief, the future, unknown and the past filled with everything from the present and future to remember and learn from.

The formation of a thought can heighten all of the senses abandoned by laziness.

The electricity of a thought can be that lightning bolt of inspiration that fuels the outpouring of a great idea.

The future is blocked by an awkward silence desperate to be heard and an unknown passage waiting to be uncovered.

What's the point in eating natural foods, naturally made, with natural ingredients, when all that happens is you die of natural causes?

A second marriage is a complete indictment on the stupidity of doing it the first time.

The whole truth is often found hidden behind half baked lies

Toothache is the pain that drives you to extraction

Is tomorrow the greatest labor saving device of today?

WHY IS IT THAT YOU FORGET
THE THINGS YOU WANT TO REMEMBER
BUT REMEMBER THE THINGS YOU WANT TO FORGET?

The biggest loser in the food chain is a chicken, eaten before birth and then again after death!

If a piece of beef or a whole chicken cost $5 in Safeway, how much is a human life worth lying dead on a battlefield?

Do most cows end up as hamburger meat because they have no steak in their future?

A yawn is an open expression of opinion doled out honestly and liberally at every occasion

A committee is a body of people that keeps minutes and wastes hours.

The exception to the rule is always the rule of exception.

Why fix it if it isn't broken? So, what's better, the fix or the change? Ask an addict!

Until you sleep in dreams alone, true friends never seemed so close.

Love is a gift - you can't buy it, you can't earn it, you can't find it...someone has to give it to you.

Happiness, is not doing the job you want to do...it's doing the job you DON'T want to do, then having done it - that is real happiness.

Each day you should fill your soul with all of life's beauty so that in death it's remembered for it's beautiful life.

Carrying that torch from generation to generation does nothing but illuminate that fire inside, which is continuous failure

IS MY INSANITY A BY-PRODUCT
OF THE KNOWLEDGE I CAPTURE
AND THEN CHOOSE TO IGNORE?

With the understanding of it's meaning comes the complete acceptance of the certainty of death

A churning mind is the catalyst for insomnia but the gateway to future success or resolution

Too much alcohol can turn simple words into incredible thoughts that eventually wear off into a sobering reality

It's completely insane when insanity can be used as a plausible defense against the abuse of sanity.

The quickest way to find something you have misplaced and been searching for is to go out and buy a replacement.

The only thing guaranteed predictable is the unpredictable.

A secret is something you quietly whisper to one person at a time.

A secret is something never spoken out loud but quietly passed between large mouths and ever lager ears.

If you are told you only have 6 weeks to live, does that mean you have less time to worry about when you are going to die?

The only way that modesty can travel is incognito

Selflessness can often alter one's ability to be completely understood.

Is the subconscious conscious or subconsciously unconscious?

Being politically correct means that true feelings are often hidden behind rehearsed words

Forgiveness is a huge word, being able to be forgive is beyond words, being forgiven requires words, none of which should be unforgivable.

IF LOVE CAN BE FELT ON ALL DIMENSIONS,
IS IT AS MUCH IN THE MIND AS IT IS IN THE HEART?

Life is always uncertain and unpredictable whereas death is always certain and completely predictable.

A lie is just a plate glass window that can be seen through by anyone with enough intelligence.

When you are foolish enough to stretch a lie too far, intelligent people see through it.

When times are tough, look to your past and remember they were not always that way and then think about your future and hope that good times will again make you smile with even fonder memories.

Ambition of the most powerful is fueled by their desire to uncontrollably dictate and rule the masses

Worry is an inconvenient diversion from the calmness of serenity, which when rationalized logically, is just a moment in time that is disturbing, creating longer periods of inconvenience.

The pain that comes from a broken heart is not nearly as vicious as the self-inflicted hatred that comes from that pain.

An unsettled argument followed by extended silence is a catalyst for the demise of friendship

Words are not only powerful when spoken, but sometimes more meaningful when kept silent

It's great to be opinionated, as long as that opinion is not inflicted with any ill intent on anyone who chooses to remain open minded.

If it was not for the creation of liberty and those who fought for it, my ancestral lineage would have been terminated and thus my birth non-existent.

The folly of another mans war is the uncomfortable reminder found inside a different man's wallet.

THE GIFT OF TIME
IS THE PRESENT OF EVERY MOMENT.

A flight of fancy is more often than not a fanciful excursion to a destination called failure

The difference between dreaming in life and dreaming whilst sleeping is fulfillment. In sleep there are no expectations.

It's never fashionable to be late, but it does set a trend to arrive early.

Being accused of having no balls is not the end of one's sexuality but more the beginning of a journey to recover one's self esteem.

The only part of life that's under complete control is destiny.

The only thing in life that you can control, good, bad or indifferent, is your own behavior.

Every split second is the presence of a future moment

Every split second is the future of a present yet unknown.

Election results can be swung not by those who vote, but by those who don't.

Elections are never rigged; they are only manipulated by those who choose that those who voted have as much say as those who didn't.

Is it responsible to be irresponsible in order to learn the true meaning and value of responsibility?

A man who decides to build higher than the last and without conviction or gratitude to the heavens will end up lower than most begging for relief and restitution

You end up where you came from, not knowing where you are.

TELL ME WHAT IS HONESTY
AND I'LL SHOW YOU WHAT IS TRUTH.

The greatest gift one human being can give another is total respect

There should be no tolerance given to those who are intolerant

There is no natural cure for nature, only the acceptance of her greatness and appreciation of her indiscriminate powers

Knowledge, which comes from education and experience, is a gift, a gift to be used wisely.

A momentous event is not necessarily eventfully momentous although it could be momentously eventful

Is a jet-lagged mind inflamed by the fuel from travel or just traveling on mindless inflammation?

My life would have been very ordinary but for those who have lived it with me and made it extraordinary

Terrorist threats cannot be eliminated by terrorizing
a terrorist and indeed we can probably
only terminate terror by the acceptance that
the terrorist is never terrified to torment and terrify
until he is terrified by continual torment.

If getting old means slowing down then does speeding up slow down the aging process?

If you type a letter while sitting nude in front of the computer, does it give the content more feeling?

If you sit at the computer completely nude typing a letter or email does that make the content more intimate?

Is an accent handed down or picked up?

AGEING IS JUST THE COUNTDOWN TO DEATH,
CELEBRATED BY A DAY OF ANNUAL HAPPINESS.

Work is a four-letter word, but only for those who cannot spell.

The grass is always greener, but only if you know how to cut it

The time to become adventurous is when you can afford to do it first class.

If life is so short, then why does it take us so long to live it?

I practice religion like I practice safe sex, as little possible, or not at all, with the sensation of true feelings vented in the fact that both are complicated, both generally have happy or sad endings, depending on the timing of the climax and conviction of belief.

If there is always a before and an after but the after is no better than the before should the before be after the after or should the after remain after the before?
For a happy ever after?

Everyone is the architect of their own fortune but those born wealthy are given greater planning permission

Can a dog cat nap?

Is it too much to imagine that the power of thought brings with it thoughtful imagination?

Is it a stretch of the imagination to consider that the power of thought is not an imaginary glitch of powerful misinterpretation?

Trust fund babies are born as rich adults

Reality is the ultimate form of all speculation

If reality is the ultimate form of speculation, should speculation ever be considered as a possibility?

IF SARCASM IS THE LOWEST FORM OF WIT
THEN TO BE FUNNY
DO YOU NEED TO BE SINCERE?

The secret of success is not always found in the planning, but in the execution of a plan that is successful.

If your persistently consistent does that mean your persistence is consistently constant?

Alcoholism is a fine line driven between indulgence exuberance and ignorance.

Alcoholism is an indulgence which divides a fine line between genius and stupidity.

Is a formidable force forcefully formidable or formidably forceful?

The good in me is humbled by the great in you.

When a starving man asks for more, it's considered greed, when a rich man takes more, it's considered to be his right

When a poor man goes for second helpings, it is considered the greed of a glutton.

When a rich man has a four-course meal, it is considered quality of living.

Is the silence of fear worse than the sound of terror? OR found in terror

Is being terrified of fear worse than being fearful of terror?

You have to experience the nightmare of a dream before you can enjoy the reality of success

The finish line is always further than the start but to start you have to finish first

DO YOU HAVE TO DO WHAT YOU WANT TO DO
OR SHOULD YOU WANT TO DO WHAT YOU HAVE TO DO?

Waiting for death is like waiting for a bus, it shows up unexpectedly and never when you want it

Getting old is one of life's cruelest tricks, dying young robs you of any of the magic of growing old and both are just illusions in a game filled with jokers with no ace up your sleeve to prolong survival

The angel of death has no wings, only bullets

When one life ends, another begins, therefore why isn't each ending celebrated by a new beginning instead of mourned like a dead loss?

To fully appreciate the dream, you have to first live the nightmare

Life is all 'Don't Knows" Don't know when you are conceived, don't know when you are born, don't know what day or time you will die, don't know what happens next, don't know if I like that and don't know if I have a choice.

A recession is when some of your friends lose their jobs. A depression is when you lose yours!

The end of a relationship is like the end of the alphabet, she is your x and then you ask y every night before you get some z's

Recession leads to depression and then discretion overrules regression, leading back to expression of expansion.

Your forehead is the perfect device for finding furniture in the dark

Anonymity does not necessarily bring with it the gift of peace

The early bird always gets the worm. But the second mouse always gets the cheese on the trap

AS AN ARTIST THERE ARE JUST PICTURES,
IMAGES OF HOW LIFE SHOULD BE,
WHICH ARE PURE FANTASY AND ABSOLUTE REALITY.

The greatest power a man possesses is to kill and take another mans life, the greatest gift a man can give, is sparing that life.

The only helping hands you never want to rely on, are the one's that lower your coffin into the ground!

The grass may be greener on the other side of the fence, but it is just as hard to cut/water.

To keep children's' feet on the ground it helps if you put added responsibility on their shoulder

Crime is born from poverty or greed and its criminal to be greedy and poor.

In the race to achieve all your dreams, which wins, the probability, the possibility or the accomplishment?

The magnitude of any disaster can be measured, not by the number of lives lost, but by the number still alive who cared

Does a dream commence when you shut your eyes or when you open your mind?

"You are what you eat. You become what you think."

You do not have to be great to get started. But you do have to start to be great

In life you deserve no more and no less than what you are prepared to tolerate

A fulfilled life comes not from the breaths you took in, but from the memorable moments that took your breath away.

SELDOM COULD THE PLIGHT OF SO FEW HAVE CAPTURED
THE HEARTS OF SO MANY
IN SUCH A SHORT SPACE OF TIME THAT LIVES ON FOREVER.

When you win a war, the battle is just beginning, when you lose a war, someone else's battle is about to begin

Living with the fear of death is just a frightening as dying with the fear of living

All of the world's greatest achievements were accomplished by people not intelligent enough to know they were impossible

Those unfortunates homed in cardboard boxes, have always firmly believed the road to success is still under construction

The timeline for tomorrow is now, before yesterday catches up with this present moment.

A genuine friend is one who in hard times walks in when everyone else has walked out

The road between today and tomorrow is littered with twists and turns, but the road to eternity has no stop signs and is a direct route.

A great friendship is worth every penny, as long as no money changes hands.

Is it more painful to be stabbed in the back, shot through the heart, or just told the truth?

Sanity, it's nothing but a dream played out by experience!

Life is not measured by the number of breaths we take in, it is measured by those moments that take our breath away

A sudden death not on your calendar becomes an appointment impossible to miss.

The probability of affability comes from dependability and accessibility.

Does authority evolve from responsibility or is it just responsible to be authoritative?

IS DUTY MORE IMPORTANT THAN DESIRE
OR IS IT DESIRABLE TO BE DUTIFUL?

It truly is better to give than to receive, unless receiving is a giving experience

You were born with a great memory, so don't ever forget it.

The art of conversation comes from a canvas full of words and a pallet replenished by colorful thoughts

If you spend your life dreaming of the person you would like to be, do you leave behind the person you really are?

When dreams come true were they really dreams at all or just expectations?

I have no fight with God, just issues with those who claim to represent him.

Can commitments to deadlines be ignored for deadlines with commitments?

We come a long way from where we were born but we are always very close to where we will die

Time heals everything, except the loss of time itself

Do the pictures turning round in your head leave you with any words that make sense?

I could be a lot of things, but I can only ever be me

All gay people should be allowed the rights of marriage, so that they too can experience the confusion and stress all the rest of us have to put up with

If safety always comes first, what comes second?

Whoever said that freedom of speech was an inalienable right was obviously a bachelor TV

From dirt to flesh, all we are is a reflection of the heavens

THE PROBLEM WITH GOVERNMENT TODAY IS THAT IT'S FILLED
WITH A BUNCH OF DO-GOODERS,
DOING NO GOOD AT ALL.

Freedom costs more than just a lot of money, but captivity is and expense we can live without.

In life, those who cut corners end up running round in circles

Even the wisest of men will never see anything in their own shadow?

The pleasure from a joyful emotional experience can be felt in your heart but never touched in your mind

Beautiful gardens blossom not only from an abundance of water, but also from an abundance of perspiration.

A man with a closed mind can only be educated by another with an open heart.

An overwhelming challenge should always be seen as an incredible opportunity never a distraction or impossibility.

Pride should come from within the soul and not before sampling both victory and defeat in the same body.

Life is but a fleeting glimpse into what the great unknown has to offer

The act of dying is something that clearly frightens me and is something in which I have no intention to participate, unless it becomes meaningful and necessary.

Being an unwilling participant, I am sadly forced into submission by a force greater than that of any living mind or body, though hopefully with an invigorated spirit, willing to rise again amongst nurtured souls.

It may take an eternity for you to love someone unconditionally but it takes unconditional love to complete eternal time.

Unconditional love should be given as well as taken, time should never be taken, just loved unconditionally.

Every second of gifted time is the present that no one will die for.

The only cure for the fear of taking after one's father, is not knowing who he was in the first place.

Guilt stems from your own inability to accept and reconcile the imbalance of wealth on this planet and the acknowledgement that you have succeeded by chance and by desire where other's have not

Wisdom is the ability to foresee what blinds others.

Life is important only to those who take death seriously

If I did everything I could do or was supposed to do, I'd never get anything done at all.

Are bad habits habit forming if they form habits that are informally bad?

If you rise to the bait does that mean you're another fish out of water or just another fool who cannot swim?

Silence can be deafening but it is always golden and can never be misquoted.

Nothing lasts forever, even the knowledge of that certainty.

If you don't make the effort to change it then tomorrow will be just like today.

Expectation is an open gateway to failure and disappointment.

Grief is everyone's rite of passage from the reality of a finality to the finality of that reality.

To learn from someone who is all-alone is to understand solitude and the desire to be accepted.

Madness is a surrogate of eccentricity, which in turn gives birth to genius.

This moment is all but a memory that flashes by and then becomes the past.

The Day begins with silence and then a deep breath and after many experiences ends with the same silence and yet another deep breath

Dreams are only worth the wasted imagination it takes to concoct them

The purpose of ambition is to sustain a continual thirst for life that should never die

Ambition is a catalyst that enhances the desire to stay alive

There's your choice, there's my choice and then there's no choice at all.

In the beginning there's an end but in the end, there's no beginning.

There are no days off, only the possibility of failure for not showing up

The certain thing about being certain is the uncertainty that makes being certain the only uncertain thing.

The happiest people are those who realize that unhappiness is a state of mind to be admonished

Is satisfaction guaranteed in a society where guaranteed satisfaction is never satisfying enough?

Everyone seems to have something to say, but no one seems to have anything to do.

Addiction is possessing an addictive additive that no addict wants to be addicted to.

The greatest lapse of judgement is making a judgement call and then letting it lapse.

Each disrespected sunrise and sunset are proof that life matters little and that time is taken for granted.

It's nice to be nice rather than not nice because being not nice is not nicer than nice.

www.ingramcontent.com/pod-product-compliance
Lightning Source LLC
Chambersburg PA
CBHW040932030426
42336CB00001B/6